A PORTRAIT IN POEMS

The Storied Life of GERTRUDE STEIN & ALICE B. TOKLAS

written by
Evie Robillard

illustrated by
Rachel Katstaller

Kids Can Press

To Kurt and Tammi — and their puppies, Jake and Paloma — E.R.
For my family. And Hemingway, of course. — R.K.

Acknowledgments

Thanks so very much to: Kathleen Keenan, editor — thoughtful, perceptive, tactful.
Abigail Samoun — for finding the perfect home for this story, and for being wise enough to
invite Rachel Katstaller to illustrate it. I'm also grateful to the entire editorial and production
staff at Kids Can Press, and for Greta Schiller's documentary *Paris Was a Woman*. — E.R.

Kids Can Press gratefully acknowledges the financial support of the
Government of Ontario, through Ontario Creates; the Ontario Arts Council;
the Canada Council for the Arts; and the Government of Canada for our
publishing activity.

Text excerpts are printed with permission from the Estate of
Gertrude Stein, through its Literary Executor, Mr. Stanford Gann, Jr.,
of Levin & Gann, P.A.

Published in Canada and the U.S. by Kids Can Press Ltd.
25 Dockside Drive, Toronto, ON M5A 0B5

Kids Can Press is a Corus Entertainment Inc. company

www.kidscanpress.com

The artwork in this book was rendered in gouache, colored pencils and graphite.
The text is set in Colby.

Edited by Kathleen Keenan
Designed by Marie Bartholomew

Printed and bound in Shenzhen, China, in 10/2019 by C&C Offset

CM 20 0 9 8 7 6 5 4 3 2 1

Library and Archives Canada Cataloguing in Publication

Title: A portrait in poems : the storied life of Gertrude Stein and Alice B. Toklas /
written by Evie Robillard ; illustrated by Rachel Katstaller.

Other titles: Storied life of Gertrude Stein and Alice B. Toklas

Names: Robillard, Evie, author. | Katstaller, Rachel, illustrator.

Identifiers: Canadiana 20190099194 | ISBN 9781525300561 (hardcover)

Subjects: LCSH: Stein, Gertrude, 1874–1946 — Juvenile literature. | LCSH: Toklas,
Alice B — Juvenile literature. | LCSH: Authors, American — 20th century —
Biography — Juvenile literature. | LCSH: Stein, Gertrude, 1874–1946 — Friends
and associates — Juvenile literature.

Classification: LCC PS3537.T323 Z856 2019 | DDC j818/.5209 — dc23

Table of Contents

... writers have to have two countries, the one where they belong and the one in which they live really.

— Gertrude Stein, *Paris France*

27 RUE DE FLEURUS

The next time you go to Paris,
you might visit this big green spot
on your map: the Luxembourg Gardens —
or Jardin du Luxembourg. And right there,
in the middle of the garden,
is an eight-sided pond
where you can rent a tiny sailboat
and set it adrift over and over again.

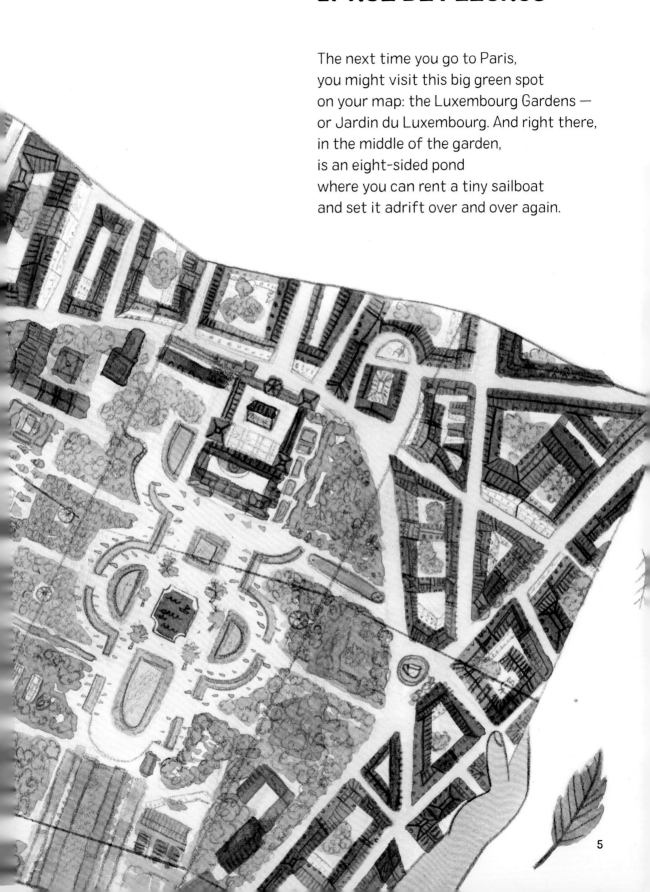

Just west of the pond
is a little street — or, as French people say,
a *rue*. Rue de Fleurus, it's called. And there,
at 27 rue de Fleurus, is a place that once was filled with paintings —
bright, bold, wild, impossible paintings.

And in that place lived a woman named Gertrude Stein
and her brother Leo.
And, later on, her partner, Alice.

Gertrude didn't *paint* the paintings
that hung on the walls at 27 rue de Fleurus.
Neither did Leo.
So, how did they get there?

Gertrude and Leo bought them,
one by one, after they moved to Paris.
Paris was the home of many artists.
The shops and galleries
were filled with work by:

Matisse, Cézanne, Gauguin,
Marie Laurencin,
Georges Braque, Juan Gris.
And, of course, *Picasso.*
The one and only Pablo Picasso.

Her feet are too flat, if you ask me.

I talk French badly and write it worse, but so does Pablo . . .

— Gertrude Stein, *Everybody's Autobiography*

PICASSO PAINTS A PORTRAIT

Leo loved the work of Pablo Picasso.
Picasso had moved to Paris from Spain in 1900,
just a few years before Gertrude.

But which of his paintings
should they buy?

Finally, Leo chose one.
Gertrude *almost* liked it.

And then they invited the artist to dinner.

Gertrude sat next to Pablo that night.
And when she reached for a piece of bread,
he grabbed it away from her.

"This piece of bread is mine!" he said.

Gertrude laughed
and Pablo's face turned red. And suddenly
he was asking if he could *please please please*
paint her portrait,
and Gertrude was saying *yes. Yes, I suppose so.*

Before long
Gertrude was walking each morning
up rue des Saints-Pères,
crossing a bridge over the Seine
and then climbing the long, slow hill
to the artist's studio in Montmartre.

Pablo studied her with his wild, dark eyes.
Eyes that took in everything. And then
he began to paint. Eighty times
during the winter of 1906,
Gertrude climbed that hill
and sat quietly
while Pablo painted
& painted
   & painted.

Until one day he said,
"I can't see you anymore when I look!"
And he did *this* to the canvas!

But one day that summer —
voilà!

Just like that —
without even asking Gertrude to sit for him —
he finished the painting!

Gertrude was very pleased with it,
so he gave it to her as a gift.
And she kept it forever.

And, one more happy thing —
not long after that, Alice B. Toklas arrived in Paris.
On her second day in the city, she met Gertrude Stein.
And in a very short time they were inseparable.

Little by little people began to come to the rue
de Fleurus to see the Matisses and the Cézannes...
and they came at any time and it began to be a nuisance,
and it was in this way that Saturday evenings began.

— Gertrude Stein, *The Autobiography of Alice B. Toklas*

SATURDAY EVENINGS

Now, if you wanted to meet Gertrude Stein —
to see the many paintings that she
and Leo had bought —
you'd need to ring the bell
at 27 rue de Fleurus.

The door would open
and a tiny, dark-haired woman —
Alice B. Toklas —
would let you in. She'd offer you
a cucumber sandwich,
or one of her delicious cakes,
and, of course, a cup of tea.

While you were sitting in the kitchen,
Alice would ask you lots of questions
in her quick, quiet voice. She'd want to know
where you went to school
and which books you liked to read . . .
which artists were your very favorite
and what you wanted to do when you grew up.

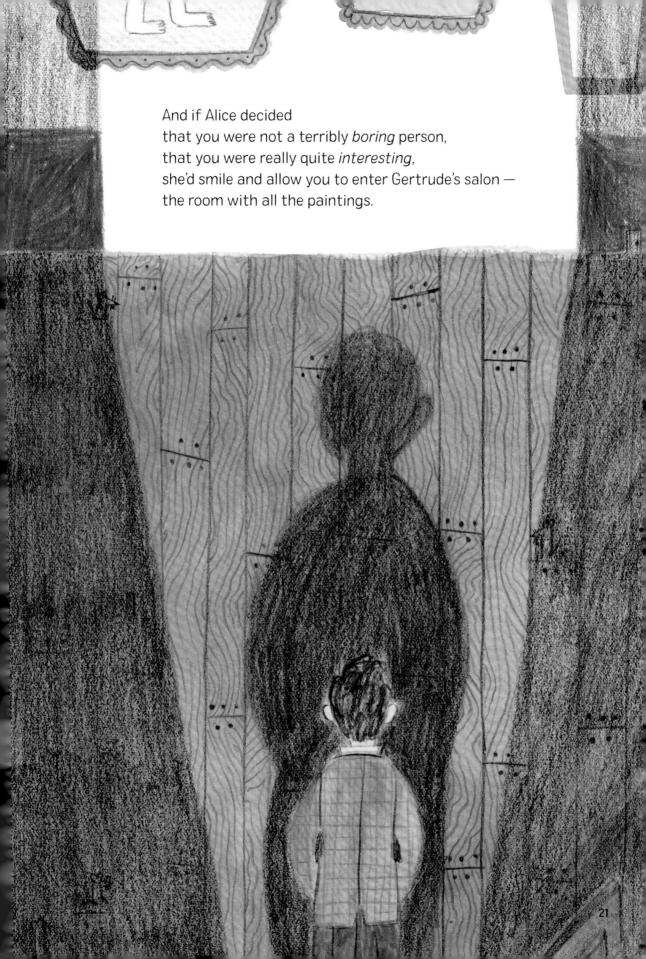

And if Alice decided
that you were not a terribly *boring* person,
that you were really quite *interesting*,
she'd smile and allow you to enter Gertrude's salon —
the room with all the paintings.

You know how painters are,
I wanted to make them happy . . .
they were happy so happy we had
to send out twice for more bread.

— Gertrude Stein, *The Autobiography of Alice B. Toklas*

THE ROOM WITH ALL THE PAINTINGS

Look at all these people!
Sipping tea and drinking wine
and *oohing*
and *aahing*
and trying to say intelligent things
about the paintings on the walls.

Actually, some of the people might be laughing.
Or scratching their heads.
Or saying the paintings are *hideous*.

These people would probably *not*
be invited back to 27 rue de Fleurus.

Disgusting!

Ridiculous!

And *you*?
Perhaps you would enjoy Gertrude's rich, warm voice and her sudden, musical laughter.
Perhaps you'd even like the paintings!

Gertrude knew when a painting had something special to say.
Because she was Gertrude Stein.
Gertrude Stein, the genius.

Outrageous!

It takes a lot of time to be a genius,
you have to sit around so much
doing nothing, really doing nothing.

— Gertrude Stein, *The Autobiography of Alice B. Toklas*

GERTRUDE STEIN, THE GENIUS

Gertrude Stein was much, much more
than a collector of paintings
or a nibbler of tea cakes
or a person who may
or may not
invite you to see the art
on her walls.

Gertrude Stein was
a writer.

Night after night,
year after year,
she scribbled her words
into little blue notebooks —
the kind French children used in school,
and still use today.

Gertrude made up her own rules
about grammar & spelling & punctuation.
She didn't care much about periods
or commas or capital letters.
(You get to do that when you're a grown-up.
It isn't fair, but that's the way it is.)

Here is part of a poem Gertrude wrote
for her friend Pablo:

If I Told Him
A Completed Portrait of Picasso
by Gertrude Stein

If I told him would he like it.
Would he like it if I told him.
Would he like it would Napoleon
would Napoleon would would he
like it.

If Napoleon if I told him if I
told him if Napoleon. Would he
like it if I told him if I told him
if Napoleon. Would he like it if
Napoleon if Napoleon if I told him.
If I told him if Napoleon if
Napoleon if I told him. If I told
him would he like it would he like
it if I told him.

Perhaps Gertrude wrote the poem in her head
while she was sitting quietly in Pablo's studio.
After all, *she* was an artist, too.
Her poems were *more* than poems.
"Word portraits" is what she called them.

Gertrude scribbled her words.
And Alice typed them up.
And they *never* threw anything away.
They kept it all in a cabinet,
and as the years went by
the cabinet grew very full.

Gertrude didn't always write for grown-ups.
She wrote for children, too:

I am Rose my eyes are blue
I am Rose and who are you
I am Rose and when I sing
I am Rose like anything.

— *The World Is Round*

And,

Everything begins with A.
What did you say. I said everything
begins with A and I was right and hold
me tight and be all right.

— *To Do: A Book of Alphabets and Birthdays*

And here are the most famous words
Gertrude ever wrote:

Rose is a rose is a rose is a rose.

I am I because my little dog knows me.

— Gertrude Stein, *Everybody's Autobiography*

A DOG NAMED BASKET

It happened one day
when Gertrude and Alice
were walking the streets of Paris . . .

They came upon a dog show.
And one little blue-eyed puppy
barked a friendly *hello,*
wagged his tail
and jumped into Gertrude's lap.

Alice thought he was pretty enough
to carry a basket of flowers in his mouth.
So they named him Basket.

They took him home and, naturally,
they kept him.

Sometime after that,
the man who owned 27 rue de Fleurus
told Gertrude & Alice they'd need to find
a new place to live.
His son wanted to live there.

They found an apartment nearby — at 5 rue Christine.
Gertrude bought some pretty wallpaper
with fat white pigeons in a soft-blue sky.

Before long, Gertrude & Alice & Basket —
and all the paintings —
were very much at home.

And guess what?
Gertrude decided that the sound of Basket
drinking from his water dish
taught her the difference between

sentences and
paragraphs.

lap lap lap

laplaplaplaplap

laplaplaplaplap

laplaplaplaplap

I am a pretty good housekeeper and a pretty good gardener and a pretty good needlewoman and a pretty good secretary and a pretty good editor and a pretty good vet for dogs and I have to do them all at once ...

— Gertrude Stein, *The Autobiography of Alice B. Toklas*

GERTRUDE & ALICE & BASKET IN A BOOK

"Alice," said Gertrude one day.
"You live an interesting life.
You live here in Paris with me.
You know a lot of artists and writers.
You were even in the San Francisco earthquake.
Why don't you write your autobiography?"

But Alice was far too busy to write a book.
So Gertrude decided to write it for her.
She called it *The Autobiography of Alice B. Toklas*.
But it's really the autobiography of —
guess who?

Gertrude Stein.

Gertrude scribbled away
for six weeks
in their summer home in the country.
Alice typed it up
and sent it to a publisher.

And then one day
when Gertrude & Alice & Basket
were taking a walk past their favorite bookstore,
they were more than a little delighted
to see a window filled filled filled
with the book that would make them famous.
The book about their lives
and the room with all the paintings.

12

12 | SH

LENDING
LIBRARY

38

It is hard to go on when you are nearly there . . .

— Gertrude Stein, *The World Is Round*

AFTER

Gertrude Stein died in 1946.
She had been ill for months.
Even Alice's cooking could not save her.

Gertrude was buried
in Père Lachaise Cemetery.

Alice lived on
for a long time
at 5 rue Christine.
She had Basket II for company.
And, of course, the paintings.
They were worth a *lot* of money by then.

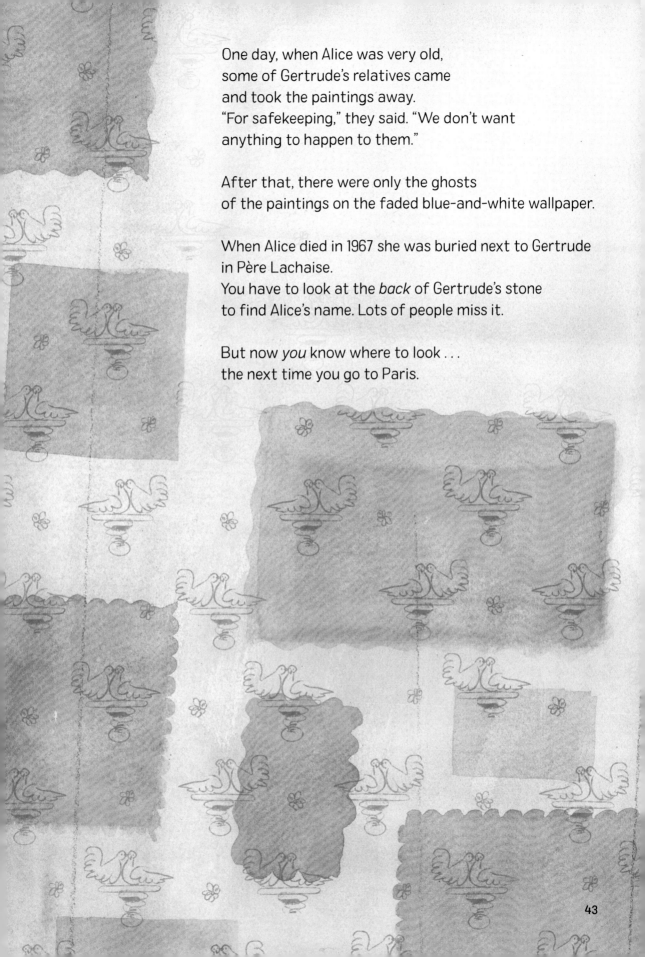

One day, when Alice was very old,
some of Gertrude's relatives came
and took the paintings away.
"For safekeeping," they said. "We don't want
anything to happen to them."

After that, there were only the ghosts
of the paintings on the faded blue-and-white wallpaper.

When Alice died in 1967 she was buried next to Gertrude
in Père Lachaise.
You have to look at the *back* of Gertrude's stone
to find Alice's name. Lots of people miss it.

But now *you* know where to look . . .
the next time you go to Paris.

TIME LINE

1874	Gertrude Stein — the youngest of five children — is born in Allegheny, Pennsylvania, to a wealthy family.
1877	Alice Babette Toklas is born in San Francisco, California.
1878	The Stein family moves to Austria and then France for one year.
1888	Gertrude's mother dies.
1891	Gertrude's father dies.
1893–1894	Gertrude attends Radcliffe College, studying philosophy and psychology. She begins to write essays and stories.
1897–1902	Gertrude attends Johns Hopkins School of Medicine, but eventually drops out to travel with her brother Leo.
1903	Gertrude moves to Paris and lives with Leo at 27 rue de Fleurus.
1905	Gertrude and Leo purchase their first paintings by Cézanne, Renoir and Gauguin.
1906	Pablo Picasso begins to paint Gertrude's portrait.
1907	Alice moves to Paris and meets Gertrude.
1910	Alice moves in with Gertrude, and not long after that, Leo moves out.
1914	Gertrude and Alice are in London when World War I breaks out. They finally return to Paris in the fall.
1917	Gertrude buys her first car, a Ford she names Auntie. She and Alice travel around France, delivering supplies to wounded French soldiers.
1918	World War I ends.

1928 Gertrude buys another car; they name this one Godiva. They adopt Basket, a French poodle.

1932 Gertrude writes *The Autobiography of Alice B. Toklas* — which is really the story of Gertrude's life.

1934–1935 Suddenly famous after the success of *The Autobiography of Alice B. Toklas*, Gertrude and Alice travel to the United States for the first time in thirty years. Gertrude gives lectures at dozens of American universities. She even visits the First Lady, Eleanor Roosevelt.

1938 Gertrude and Alice move to 5 rue Christine. Basket dies, and they get another white poodle and name him Basket II.

1939 World War II begins. Alice and Gertrude flee Paris and move into their country home, taking the Picasso portrait with them.

1944 After Paris is liberated, Gertrude and Alice return to 5 rue Christine. Much to their relief, all of the paintings are still on the walls.

1946 Gertrude undergoes surgery for colon cancer. She dies on July 27, at the age of 72. In October she is buried in Père Lachaise Cemetery.

1967 Alice dies on March 7. She is buried next to Gertrude in Père Lachaise — but her name is inscribed on the *back* of Gertrude's tombstone.

SNAPSHOTS

Gertrude Stein loved being photographed.
Here she is with Alice in their snazzy-jazzy Ford.
The car's name was Godiva.

Gertrude did all the driving —
but Alice liked to blow the *klaxon*.
(*Klaxon* is a funny French word for "horn.")

Once, they got a ticket
when Alice blew the klaxon
at a policeman!

Here are Alice and Gertrude
in the room with all the paintings.
Alice was a very tiny woman,
and Gertrude asked a carpenter to shorten the legs
on Alice's chair. So then, when Alice sat,
her feet could actually touch the floor.

And here is Gertrude showing off her bold new haircut.
"Cut it off," she said to Alice one day.
And Alice did. Alice cut and cut and cut
until Gertrude was happy.

SOURCES

SOME BOOKS BY GERTRUDE STEIN

The Autobiography of Alice B. Toklas. New York: Harcourt Brace, 1933.

Everybody's Autobiography. New York: Random House, 1937.

Geography and Plays. Boston: Four Seas, 1922.

Paris France. New York: Charles Scribner's Sons, 1940.

To Do: A Book of Alphabets and Birthdays. New Haven: Yale University Press, 2011.

The World Is Round. New York: Harper Design, 2013.

BIBLIOGRAPHY

Benstock, Shari. *Women of the Left Bank: Paris, 1900–1940*. Austin: University of Texas Press, 1986.

Schiller, Greta, dir. *Paris Was a Woman*. 1996; New York: Zeitgeist Video, 1997. DVD.

Souhami, Diana. *Gertrude and Alice*. London: I. B. Tauris, 2009.

Stendhal, Renate, ed. *Gertrude Stein in Words and Pictures*. Chapel Hill: Algonquin Books of Chapel Hill (Workman), 1994.

AUTHOR'S NOTE

When Germany invaded France during World War II, German officials, called Nazis, took over Paris. The Nazis and their leader, Adolf Hitler, destroyed works of art in the countries that they invaded. Some people wonder how Gertrude Stein's collection of paintings managed to survive the Nazi occupation of Paris. At the time, she and Alice lived in the countryside, away from the city. What kept the Nazis from breaking into Gertrude's Paris apartment and destroying the works of Picasso and others?

One explanation is that Gertrude's popularity helped save the paintings. She was a woman with many colorful and influential friends. A few of these friends were people we would not admire today. Several of them were known collaborators — men and women who chose not to oppose Hitler and his anti-Semitic (anti-Jewish) practices. To be a collaborator was a way to be safe from Hitler's powerful secret police, the Gestapo. Some collaborators, such as Gertrude's friend Bernard Faÿ, worked with the Nazis.

But we know now that the Gestapo did try to make off with the paintings one day in 1944, not long before Paris was liberated from the Nazis. It was likely Gertrude's neighbors — people who lived or worked in the building — and Paris police officers who came to the rescue. They told the Gestapo they could not enter Gertrude's apartment without written permission. Fortunately for art lovers everywhere, the Gestapo hadn't bothered to get a permit. And so, the paintings stayed where they belonged — on the walls of 5 rue Christine.

After Alice's death, many of the paintings, including *Young Girl with a Flower Basket*, the first Picasso painting the Steins ever bought, were purchased by wealthy art collectors, and some were later donated to museums. Today, you can see many of the paintings at museums and art galleries around the world.